THE BRIGHTER THE VEIL

THE BRIGHTER THE VEIL

LIA PURPURA

ORCHISES • WASHINGTON

Library of Congress Cataloging-in-Publication Data
Purpura, Lia. 1964-
    The Brighter the Veil / Lia Purpura.
        p. cm.
    ISBN 0-914061-56-9 (alk. paper)
    I. Title.
PS3566.U67B74 1996
811'.54—dc20   95-34708
                                            CIP

Grateful acknowledgement is made to the following
    publications where these poems have appeared:

American Poetry Review: "Self-Portrait with Scar"
The Antioch Review: "Museum Horse"
Columbia Magazine of Poetry and Prose: "Anger"
The Denver Quarterly: "Mourn That We Hear"
Fine Madness: "Little Parable for Doors"
Hayden's Ferry Review: "With the Cloud Formations"
Indiana Review: "Late Winter," "Tracking X," "Wall Cycle"
Negative Capability: "Construction"
Ploughshares: "The Brighter the Veil"
The Plum Review: "At the Rail Station," "On Wanting a Child,"
                "Ration," "Cardinal"
The Seneca Review: "A Little Singing"

My thanks to Kelly Dwyer, Jed Gaylin, and Patricia
Debney Watkins for generous help and encouragement.

Manufactured in the United States of America
Published by Orchises Press
P. O. Box 20602
Alexandria
Virginia
22320-1602
G6E4C2

For my parents

and for Jed

CONTENTS

III

I

WALL CYCLE

1

Dear Wall,
double secret
you show us
and show us
that what is out
there is what
here occurs
too.

2

The boy on the balcony
has his own secret.
His matches are hiding.
Wall, see how the window
wants to be like you
but can't. All day long
it proves, like a photo.

3

At night you mediate
the blue air, the black air.
Where you split, you bloom. We are
tired and lie down, headlong,
in the temple of the right angle
we make to you.

4

No more denying—
desire leaps over, sifts through you
meets up with the scent
of spice baking, wine poured
unto which I give thanks
and bless this food, my body,
and you, wall
who join us invisibly.

5

I know there are times
you've had enough of our searching
dark knots for familiar faces.
But wall, with you between us
we sleep more easily in strange places.

6

We who grew you from a stone
touch your face so changed by words:
wailing, berlin,
back up against a . . .
Wall, see everything you stand for?

South of Krakow in Kazimierz
circling the synagogue
named for Moses Isserles
(also called Rabbi Remu'h)
stands a high wall
of gravestones that were
gravestones first
then, torn up and walked upon,
sidewalks,
now a wall.

And after many years of searching
on their knees, heads bent close
to the stony smell
the archaeologists of morning
stood up, stood back, saw
you, oh cage with hinges gone
unfolded, outstretched
without a roof and bottomless
set forth in the world
to divide, amaze.

A HAT

Like her's, with a wide bank for prams,
coal dust and burning leaves in the air.
From all angles it resembles
a flower-seller's heavy arm around a bucket.
A drive over a mountain.
A monument and a street.
I long for the dark crescent shadow
like a smile, hitched over my face.
I've always wanted to wear one.

BUTTONS

The buttons' journey:
find a threshold,
slip over and stay put.
All day they hear
that little thread of
x-in-the-ears.

At night
each goes back
through its own darkness.
Star after star is led out.

Like in the story:
and then the sea parted
and the exiles crossed
to safety.

Lie down now, sleep,
dark knots, until
daylight floods you
with a body again.

DANDELIONS

Suns on the ground, rising and setting.
They also turn their broken beams
toward something greater.

All the green grass is like a sea around them.
When they are old they turn to stars.
We cannot pluck them from the sea

without their bodies scattering in air. We want them
gone before then. Before they turn to wishes.
So the children are no help, keep them away.

LOSING THE WATCH

Losing the watch
a bare arm turns up
and a few tiny hairs
the battery touched with its
contained, invisible flare.
It's hiding somewhere
like a big silver button
but no holes for thread,
just a rim in back
for force to hold in.

I keep checking my body
for signs of momentum.
The closest face is mine
in the mirror.

My wrist is bare.
A white band wraps around
the pulse time kept,
glares *when is dinner?*

Moments of terrible
perfume come back
and whole days
focus in the sharp,
bright noon of what now
becomes clear
was a desperate year.

Outside, birds rouse
for the nth time today,

moved by degrees
of that unknown power
to rustle,
to pull an offering free.

There's my neighbor
walking back from the bus
with a bag of groceries,
a bottle of wine
—so it's Friday, it must be
four-thirty, five.

Inside are pots, chairs,
a table and children,

uniforms dissolving in attics,

Medea, still taking her brother's hands
in a violent fit of wild devotion,

and he, just wanting to bring her back
to a time before hunger, or bells
in the head, alarms in the stomach.

ROUND

They hit him and they ran. He fell.
Beaten. Three hearts beat. They ran.
Where he had fallen his weeping turned to sand
like time in an ancient race.
His weeping was a hill they climbed. Stood on.
Thunderclouds gathered over him.
He was the clapper in the night bell. They ran.
How fast they ran on the pavement
over the sidewalk's hardened sand. He fell
beneath their blows. They ran. He was
a hill of sand where they could not build.
And when the rain came down his tongue was still.
He was a rock with water all around.

IN THE MILLINER'S SHOP

From one bolt
will come two blessings
cut and laid upon two heads.
Two heads wait
in woody silence.
The scissors that clip
and fashion the blessing
divide it up—
two yards of night
are draped and stitched.
The covered heads
spin on their axis.

Lightening strikes.
Crescents fall.
Scissors dull
and bend the blessing
until the milliner
comes close
to his own finger,
his own bone.
Quick, out of the whirlwind
come two black brims.
On the floor: snippets,
excess, tourniquets.

CONSTRUCTION

Where moss begins to split the wall
bricks step back like spectators.
Green is mixing a new tone there,
swelling concentrated
like a serious decision arrived at in a dream.

Closer to town, kiosks are wrapped with news.
After a few days, information shifts, ciphers form:
a smile and eye combination
a few words on a banner by an ear.
For years grey buildings by the river hold back
and then, saturated, faster and faster,
dogs and people stream out.

Back and forth through the park
old people do their all-day shopping.
They are bent, but not with weight.
They lead with their eyes towards the curve
of an orange, two oranges,
Valencia, the pounds, the change,
they are leashed
to the sight of the world.

SEWING

Thimble

I am all ears
so every sound
contradicts. Everything
echoes, loud
as a hammer
but I am
catching it.

Needle

As any pure moment occurs (see the shine!)
I do not happen only once,
I join the beginning and end, begin
and begin, out of myself, back into this whole
coat the mother is lengthening,
sleeve the daughter's arm is curving into.

Thread

A dangerous age
is bobbing towards me, claiming
yes, you'll go on living.
Here is a sliver of evidence,
a violent flash, the narrow cobbles
of a path. Hard to resist
the measure I am, an arm's length,

doubled. An embrace.
Now a chain.

Spool

Now it is gone and no more my job
to hold all I was given.
I am silent at the core.

Scissors

To go on
I dig in and leave
two paths —
one story and one
aftermath.

ANGER

She walks with one hand in her pocket
leading with the hidden fist.

She walks with her hand stuffed
in her pocket
the way a gangster
leads with a gun.

Her fist in the pocket of her blazer
leads her body the way a gangster
is led by a gun, a small hardness
pulling a great weight.

Through the stacks, she leads
with her fist in her pocket
the way a gangster is led by a gun
bearing down the weaker side.

In the library is a gangster.
A gangster whose gun has turned to sand
and is spilling on the floor.

The librarian will not allow this
in her library. Not the sand, the crying
or the smallness the gun resembles.

It is the gun who is the gangster then.
Without the gun, there is only a woman,
fist open, turned out of her pocket
sorting the books by number.

The gun leaves.
The gun walks like a naughty child
tight and hunched as a fist, slips by
the spot of sunlight on the gray carpet,
shines for a moment the way all guns
are brilliant little machines.

The gun is the gangster tapping down the stairs,
a child let loose by a bigger gangster,
sits quietly in the listening circle
dirty behind the ears.

TRACKING X

X loves no one not bound in the center,
wrung and uncertain.
Loves instead
one-who-marks-the-spot
and digs there.

Won't love one who falls on knees
but chooses one who leaves
a hole in the ground,
a target hit.

Cannot love one who won't drop down
on command recite
the A-Z
get up, shake hands.
Mind a wilderness contained.

Cannot love anyone who does not draw breath
at the sight of superheated knots budding,
berry-like blooming,
pod-juice letting down the sky.

I see you through a scope and sight
(a telescope's) dear prototype
refusing the surrender sign.
You're no white flag.
Your double-slash is balanced and still
as a calligraphic diving-bird-and-mountain-rising.

There's something in you
that would rather
be there.

Easiest mnemonic cure:
slash-slash to let the poison pass.
A rasp. A cough. An imperative: start here.
You're a beep in hieroglyph.

International sign that says
"this is where"
shovels in and makes it "here"
then moves on fast
to there and there.

O plan, site,
sketch you complete,
your entrances look
familiar as a door.
You key.

You resemble no face.

How else to know thee?

Colors you could be:

white as an apple, quartered and cored,
you're what's left in the air when the dicing's done.
white—cross section of an empty trough.
white—sand running through your sexual glass.
blue—as the skin of a heavy blue plum, dropped
to the ground, overcome with blue sun.

Other disguises:

— pause at a crossroads, driver deciding.
— birds at full span.
— bones of a kite.
— thatching of a nest held up to strong light.
— ticking sounds.
— ticking sounds that locate "here."
— sticks.
— crow's feet.
— a button's tongue.

Red scratch against the skin of night.
A plan for leaving the sky whole,
but.
The slide into sunset,
but more precise.
I'm sorry
to come back to all this evidence,
that I can't submit
reports about your startling beauty,
that paradox
in which you're hiding.

I end here. Your kiss
when it hit the earth
stitched lips.

MONUMENT

The idea that holds it up is solitary,
with a circumference barely thicker than the bronzed
arm of *Force* or neck of *Order* at the park's entrance.
If I could get my mind around it, here would be

a fable, a fierce weed
growing up into the stratosphere.
At the base where the thing is rooted

are the names of those who died
when the street was a field. Our father, a stone
man lives at the top and points downtown.

Green lights make him an ocean bird at night.
The war is over. By day,
he resigns and resigns. You can climb
hundreds of steps to see out his eyes.

PENNY

On one side it carries the entire house.
On the other, a portrait from the inner sanctum.
It must be wise—we let it choose
between us.

This is how we ask a question:
toss it in the air.
Each side is lit and doused,
lit and doused.
It turns over

the darkness of a pocket
and the hot noon sun.
Who wants to hear the answer
watches. Hides
their secret preference.

Go on, slap at it like a fly
or wish that lands finally
in the light.
See what you got.
Take your hand away.

AT THE RAIL STATION

When their train was late and they wanted to leave
none of them were more alike and they stood all

five in a circle at the desk for information
and were silent listening to the speakers.

And after not moving for a second they did.
They turned toward each other, they didn't speak

and turned away, left one another,
carried their bags and I saw no

decision among them, they were separate, all five
but they were not "frozen in time" or otherwise.

Dark wooden benches lined the perimeter
of the station and light from the hanging lamps

deepened the room and night came outside.
A few children stood on a bench looking out

a high window onto the tracks. And the travelers,
they were not shadows of equal length, nor brothers

and sisters under the lamps, the black timetable.
Even as they turned away they fell into a circle.

It was in the roundness of their faces, arms around
packages, shoulders hunched from the weight of bags

filled, and they were for a moment—
and it had been beautiful, hurt no one—

a loose circle, there for anyone to see
and to miss something else because of.

TELEPHONE POLES

Broad-shouldered children imitating
elephants—an arm for
a trunk, an arm for a tail.
Many elephants led in a circle, circling
our houses. There goes the parade,
over our heads. Our voices slung
over their backs like bridles. Crows
with hunks of bread balance
on those strong shoulders. The elephants
get smaller in the distance.
Only the tops of their heads are visible
down the road. They hum to themselves.
Their shadows are skinny because we forgot
to say *enough, it's late now, come in.*

II

INK-BLOT

It's a woman playing an ocean.
Then, over here, she drains the violin.

It's the head of a ram
gnawing grass,
or darkness that makes me think
locust and *damp*.

Eyes of a fly
enlarged and stretched.
Two fingertips

in a Balinese puppet dance.
I'm looking into

a pool of nerves.
I guess that makes me

the central stem.
And those dark spots

buds touching everything.
I think
I will freeze into a flower now, ok?

RATION

The dog that barks at crows
releases the roof of its heavy stars.

Soon a woman comes to her balcony
with a spoon
to dig her flowers out of early winter.
No, to grant a wish.

The plants fly down to the courtyard
on their many wings.

CORAL

A colony stopped here
and had a thought.
The stillness between thoughts
was a place of hope.

Where each pink mind
took on a body,
cities rose.
Thoughts grew there.

Thoughts rose through the green muscle of water.
Each one was bigger than the last.
It was all the water could do
to move around the corridors, exchanges, vacancies.

They settled in.
Made a crowd.
Made themselves
thought-windows and thought-doors.
A breeze. Routes out.

A LITTLE SINGING

The gate in the heart of a bush.
The door blown past its arc and stuck.
The garden undercolored in September
and the shrunken berries tart.
He was on the roof in an undershirt
hauling buckets of soot from the chimney.
One fire burning leaves.
Another for bread and sausages.
The samovar, tea with rum and cakes outside.
New wooden crosses in the forest and an anthill.
Dogs behind the gates we passed. Clear night.
The car careening. Him at the wheel.
The knowledge of a tank.
The teapot half-full.
In the morning, dried leaves in the spout and lid.
The hanging herbs, corn and red flowers.
The children's drawings pinned to the center wall.
The tub and the water drawn, twice-used.
The book that showed him with a tank.
Drying mushrooms spread on an iron grate.
In all the tiny kitchen jars,
shriveled things without resemblance.
The fire. His book.
She sat with the head of a sunflower on her lap
and pulled the seeds one at a time.
His eyes were without bitterness, he mocked nothing.
Hours of work and still not tired.
Onions and soot.
The days, the fires.
Same eyes, same onions, same dishes.
A little singing after dinner.
A little clapping.

CARDINAL

A few sounds and the vine
took it back. Gathered red
and the intention of reattaching.
Just that the bird took a mind
to fill up on red berries.
And the vine sent it out again, filled.
Saw wings, saw the stain on the beak
and the bird flying back.
Just that it wasn't finished.
And the berries disappeared,
took their ideas of ground into flight
moved fast now across days
across fields on those wings.

MOSQUITO

You test the air a long time
then go in. Bow your head,
kiss. Swallow. Hard to fly, isn't it?
From the patch behind the ear
where silence goes to wait,
where I'm sleeping, unadorned, you dig.
A little rage of memory begins.
I feel a blink
at the back of my head.
The tattoo of one eye reddens,
opens a dark reflex.

MOURN THAT WE HEAR

Mourn that she hears the familiar doorlock
unclick, and listens for it anxiously
stoic in her tucked, huge hems.
Reeling she is blown, and lands
gusted from that raving, malignant hand,

and comes to expect that one who is sick teaches sickness.
One cruel and with a bag full of that, up-ends that.
Such rain rains down, the flaming palm-print flat against
the face, meant not to heal, meant instead to startle
like the peal of a bell—such variations are prepared for.

One who is outside the window bellows.
That one wants in, to eat here, and bellows
in hunger or in anger.
Oh tell us low, riotous thing:
is there more than this, and what replenishes.

Earth, round wheel, tottering globe
sit at this table, come, folded, sit your long legs
disproportionate, under this table
and balance it, take reign,
take the head of the table.

"Something's rattling the door"
says the soothing Earth who built the knob.
"Let him in if singing softly
softly let the key-latch, hinge,
plate, tumblers
and bearings crack,

reveal the landing,
the well-worn brick path,
let him in if leading
a child over it
and if he allows the silence
the child loves
and the child to go first
and to live
in that house
without harm."

A MAN

A man walking beside a pond
is doubled.
There is the walker
and the reflected.

If a stick is thrown,
purposefully,
there is a man,
a man, a man.
Then brown at the collar,
threading away.

There is a long time
of shapes in the water.
Looking up, a high fence
and beyond, after the eye
has had enough, there
is coming back down.

At that point,
all our eyes
and eyes and eyes
watch closely
so the color
rejoins the man's neck
as a collar.

LATE WINTER

Afraid small steps won't get me there
I take the bus—two, three, ten steps at once.
I lose count.
My sudden movements are not
improvisational anymore.
Good reasons for stopping:
the sidewalk mysteries,
cracks, targets
a blue beetle navigating by the sun
are left behind.

Scenes pass more quickly this way, yes,
but still time for equations:

1: *Don't have but want.*
And there I build a pile for God.
Big pile built for hungry God,
stacks of belief and thanks
unbinned, restacked.
Pyramids of wheat in sun.

Searching, searching
(what else to give?)
a little X of fear slips in.
The equation shifts.

2: *Don't have and so don't want.*
A meager pile of reluctant gifts accumulates.
Offerings no one would miss.
Pocked stones. Dried cobs.
Hoarding a little seat by the window.

Skirting a pyre. Drawing a scarf around tighter.
Hungry God unsatisfied.

*

The bus is full today.
Children on a school trip are packed in tight
or would be running.
The bus makes a violent stop. Everyone explodes
silently inside. Women and men
with packages between their knees
surge and fall.
Some shoving but also warmth, undulation.
I locate, like a dancer
(for I have not given up my legs)
a still point
and a door.

WITH THE CLOUD FORMATIONS

First he tried
the sound of a man falling
a long way off a cliff.
The sound alone
was a long time coming.

The sky was blue
like a story repeated.
His family missed him
in the afternoon.

The cliff was listening
in its way. With two voices
he was less afraid.

Wasn't the sky today
full of motion
coming up with

second chances, living
proof through the door-frame?

His breathing
was immense and moving,

his enormous heart
so recently a bead of water,
fell and rose

and with no
effort at all
held him to it.

TIGER LILY

To the fire and its green secret,
to her spotted throat
he comes to drop
the kiss of sight in.

It is how her damp arms
bring heart's seed
to his dark eyes.
Colossal eyes.
It is how his empty hands
are scented.

ICON

His halo interrupts her's like a bite.
His raised hand is smaller than her lips, her head
inclines towards him. They are together and the
hammered vines and fleurs-de-lis are gold
around them. Stars landed on her
veil and on his hem. Pleats fold over
her shoulder and form, with tassels,
a cluster of arches the eye passes through
after touching each fastened red
and blue jewel. Her eyes are blue too.
His hair is cut short.
What does she do with such a child,
perfectly formed, with presence and visible
muscle even, his hand up to show us?
Talks with him—but listens here.
He just finished speaking, the words in air
are ancient, occur at her neck, at each ear
and over his head, like thoughts he makes
out of our stares. She's watching the distance
off to the right, over our shoulders—in
the best of all worlds . . . but he's wrapped
already in the shirt of a priest
and a blanket. He must be
standing on her lap, both feet
together the size of her knee.

BIRTHDAY IN A DIM BAKERY

Just this morning I hop to the sink
and pull a silvery light from my head.
I make a wish and lose it in air.
Go back and forth. Stay in bed?
I need my ancient aunt
to read this sign.

And just this morning
I find with my tongue
the space
that grew up overnight
between two teeth.
I can fill, empty, fill it
as I please. A gift—
the aristocratic imperfection
I've always wanted.

Then the surprise
spotlight
as I walked in.

The receipt-drawer banging shut
after an all-night, day-old sale.

The sound the register made
was light and delicate,
and numbers rang forth
in the little window,
called up by round, brass keys.

Brown paper, rolled like a torte.
A spool of waxy string, one piece
caught fast, stiff as a wick.

Sawdust and crumbs on the floor.
On a peg, a white apron
stained
with hand-prints.

Huge hands.

Not at all unappetizing.

TODAY ON MY WALK

Today on my walk I kissed the cold air.
The pursing up was familiar, dear.
The store window caught and held the trace
of a shrinking, foggy moon on glass.
When I turned, the wind lifted a crazy bouquet—
it took and rode my breath away.
Today on my walk, I kissed the cold air.
I made a bouquet because you were not there.

THERE, LOVE

There, stilled,
hummingbird or honeyed leaf?
Fast, by the road, death's come
or the black hump of a shorn wheel?
Puddle drying, or belly of sun
gutted, shining and gone?

Closer, the first oriole
we've ever seen.
Quick, love, the dark-
eyed flowering
into the trees.

III

THE BRIGHTER THE VEIL

The brighter the white veil
the more daring the modesty.
The yellower the dandelion
the more rampant the growth,
the health careening toward unveiling.
The louder the wheels
the deeper the plough sinks
in the black field.

The darker the soil, the more water it holds.
The deeper the plough, the louder the clank and whir.
The brighter the sun, the more complete
the unveiling of a yellow mustard field.
The dandelion in comparison, more daring in modesty,
careens toward its white veil.

The more receptive the field to the bright sun
the deeper in hope the plough must sink dryly.
The louder the field, the more life in it.
Silent, rampant it runs from the plough.
The more mustard grown, the yellower
the dusty wheels turn, careening
through the veil of modest growth.

The darkening sun lodges among pocked weeds.
The modest stalks in strict yellow light
become more daring now.
The darker the soil,
the louder the clicks and whirs.
The more rampant the growth
the more careening the health.

The brighter the white moon displays its white veil,
the more rampant the plough, the more modest
the yellower, the more silent, the brighter
the more dandelion, the more mustard
the field itself, deeper, the daring field
careening, the louder, the dew, the more dew
the white veil brighter, the modesty more daring.

FOR THE ROOSTER, THE YEAR

I come out of night with a sun in my head.

This year, to be silent before the morning
whose approach I measure
in my rising pulse—to be
predictable in that silence! But no
earthly diligence moves me. Torn from flight,
I'm a live weather vane. By terrible decree
I'm royalty. Not blessed
like the goat, whose shoulders are strong,
whose neck floods the ground
with all the year's secrets.
I announce the light.
My panic never leaves. My yellow lid
snaps up on a dark planet and everlastingly
I flinch. I will never be taken
by deep water or shallow water or into a gusty wind.
I will go on with my clutching, light seizing
my body, pinned to this railing, frightened
of the fire coming, frightened of the lifting
all around me, first the small cracks, then seams
gaping with red heat. If I were slower,
more desolate, like the mourning dove
who comes too late, whose alarm sounds like
the long, last days of a sad year
or a rusty wheel. . . .
How beautiful it is here. How still.
A branch of light snags like a bone.
All rise after me.

BURYING IT

Here's testament to
the astonishing truth:
you're best, old seed
in no sun at all.
Dark tear, taken in
like a burr on a cuff
you confess to the mop
you want under the stove
where drippings fall,
where burned grease lodges
dries and shatters.
You feed and hide there.
Shrivel and stall.

When my tongue touched
the bitter streak at your core
I spit you out. Almost
swallowed you,
homunculus
crouched knees-to-chest,
job for a broom,
mote of blood
waiting for breeze
or a corner
where something still
loves you.

Old growth, you live
in the pressed, tight fold
of a paper napkin.
Pushed under scraps,

waiting to be
tossed away.
Blue bruise.
Pit. Shady platelet.

Now concentrate.

I will not have you
rise again.

I make the shush of blooming as I go.

MUSEUM HORSE

Blue horse unhitched and riderless.
Mouth of greens, earth green below.
Dark eye fixed and seeing out.

Twisted, the horse
is checking behind.
Sound black in the ear, flies
clustering there.
Head so turned and held so long

should hurt like that.
Must be in pain.

The front leg shortened
by the turning neck
just stops, mid-air,

must mean *look harder* then *so close*
there's too much horse,
stand back.

And back there in the field
the yellow of provisions,
hay-like ochers, browns and stalks
are stacked in bales far off,

the horse bluer now
against it all, against the pale sky
that yields to the horse.

If the air is warmer
below the line of dipping belly
then hoof lift up and stay mane shining!
Dark mane bloom back, tick against
the listening ears, and light underfoot
where nothing rests

now cobble up.
Make the pause
less cruel.

BOUNTY

In the beginning, Domenico Ghirlandaio
painted with oil on wood
a tree, chapel, rocky mountain, winding road
framed by a window beyond the seated
Old Man and Boy, the old man
with a bulbous, deformed nose and the child
adoring in a red cap with gold curls.
Here the question of beauty fades—it's not exactly
that I forget you're there, holding out
the tiny girlish hands you'll never ruin, since
dressed as you are, with such a view,
brocade at your collar, the heavy work
is left to others—but it's his face
I keep returning to, shamelessly
centered, exceptionally touched
with pinks and browns. I cannot stop looking
at his love for you, at your perfect face,
at your love for his other perfection, that center,
no one then or now is able to rest from.

DOUBTFUL ASSUMPTION

I, who believed in paying with my body
as if directly to the pocket of God
with the coins of my days,
with the muscles of my back
wilting under the angry shirt,
with the muscles of my eyes, weak
from the horizon's refusal
to feed such a gaze,
sacks over shoulders
and hands folded,
I knew my complicity in others'
rage, uncertainty, isolation.

To convince them otherwise was easy.

My perfection is their icon,
their flawless bead, their love
not for themselves,
but for their earth,
capable of sustaining someone
so unlike them,
yet in a house among them.

What do they imagine I do at night
or when I wake, early, with the weight
of my own good intentions and the memory
of my vivid failures?
Do they suppose that I have never
walked directly into danger
after seeing every warning,

that in the midst of a friend's confusion
I did not enjoy the sanctuary
of my own clear intellect,
not having been chosen
for her particular agony?

They cannot know
if this confession
is in itself a whole effort
or merely a quarter-turn into the light
so they might view it partially,
as they want to anyway:
a bright, confident choice, wholly just
and delivered from a difficult past.
Bound by rules of form,
they cannot know
if I am holding
more light still.

Some days I feel I am
a distant arrival point,
a busy, one-way route or animal,
ears pitched forward, listening,
led directly to this spot.
In truth, I was
distracted along the way,
and my sadness has become
familiar as a meditation
or stolen coin, not spent
but held, the thought
of returning it someday
more satisfying
than ever doing so.

I am pictured now
in various stages of my life
with the tools of my good works:
anchor, basket of flowers,
bell, cauldron, hatchet,
fountain, stars
in books, on wood, walls, windows.

But my own icon, reflected,
does not reveal deeds or aspirations.
Sharp as the tine of a fork
or a splinter,
stubborn as snagged thread
or a fracture in glass, holding,
it is a trail or fuse
going in, predicting,
like the particles of my body,
a sure explosion. It is
mysterious, this gap
or parted curtain, this
smile of mine.

OWL

Because I cannot be forgiven for this rage
I will stand below it, face tilted
with a crick in my neck, for hours and believe
the rustling and three-note call.
Here I am closest to its hard claws,
they are so big, my head bows down now
in thanks because sometime soon it will act out
lifting and flying with its body.

Owl of my rage, fat as a barrel,
your yellow eyes see
how much goodness I refuse.
For hours—and I wanted it to be that long—
I walked around the block, the next block.
I had been wronged. I didn't want to stop walking.
I will tell you I had been deceitful too,
and didn't want to stop.
I walked striking the ground with my heels.
I would have pulled up weak trees with my hands
but the owl was on the highest steady branch of an oak
that reached half over the street. Buses passed
and more cars than usual—it was Friday night
and the town was going out. I would have gone home,
I would have hurt my hands more than I did,
then been disgusted at my lack of imagination.
But I found the owl, motionless.
And motionless was what I wanted—to be still
long enough to cast my silence and interrupt
that force. The owl was so still
I believed the sternness and the judgment.
It didn't move at all, except to blink.

It did that only once
and then the darkness was complete.
People passing looked up where I was looking,
saw nothing and had to ask. So I pointed and said
"there's an owl in that tree."
I emphasized *owl* first, then after a while,
because no forgiveness at all was coming, I'd say
"there's an owl in *that tree*," because
there it was, in front of my house,
in front of me.

A LITTLE TALK WITH DR. FAUST

Tired. Swallowed your stethoscope.
Now tired of those pylorean rhythms,
Tyrolean colors of bile and lobes—the revelation
of a closed system, clicking, turning without you.

What next—rob a bank? Come out with a gold brick
under your arm, with emerald and ruby-eyed
toads from the safety boxes of old people?
So were last century's finest moments worn.

Try Love. That musky smell.
Hair the color of climbing bittersweet.
Which turns to ash. Which burns off.
Like an induced state of panic or devotion.
Mysterious as the first eater of the artichoke.

What is your mission here, in this
(what to call it?) misty-frankness, starry candor?
This sullen place of titanic boredom,
this gorgeous moment, this earth, this day:

To give up hiding your ambition, your disease?

To bet the whole farm—the wily dog,
dancing goats, two-headed chickens
—just to keep them together? Oh, after all,
good hearted?

To grow? To grow old? To slip
longing under your tongue

and sit with the minty burn
and sweet decay?

In blindness to slip into the sea
faster now than the sea itself,
to slip into its dark purse,
its silk-lined, sow's ear
of a purse?

X STUDY

When x loved me
I loved x and the water on all sides,
ocean and x together like that.

I loved the grassy world
and the watery world with x.
Only years later could I pull
x-weeds from the air.

Once I missed x so much
I planted along the bare roadside
an x-ing place, while at night,
overhead, grew stars of weeds,
x-roots searching water.
That time was not brief.
There was x after x,
the slash-slash of underbrush
before the cipher of a wave
meant anything to me.
I have the x to prove it.

When x loves me now
I have a stick and the sand.
I work fast when the water
rolls back a minute.

SELF-PORTRAIT WITH SCAR

I took this line from a black-eyed susan,
all those toothy, broken petals—and this
from the jawbone of a calf, dried, on my desk.
This angle's the sun stretched over the grass
into tall shadows, the way months pass.
Here's a plunging motion, like hands underwater,
cold and slowed down.
Here was a long winter.
Here light comes off the grass in patches.
Here's the stiff coil of a rope after rain.
This dark center starts the place I can't see,
moves into a curve beyond the frame
where I left my body in someone's hands,
where a thread from elsewhere looked and came in.

ON WANTING A CHILD

With the toe of one stitch to the other's heel,
the needle of blood tightens its loop.

Slow thought where the bright needle circles,
the thought of your hair gives off sparks that linger.

The end of each day is a net to catch you.
In time, a good heft in my hand, your weight,
your finger in my slack light will snag.
Your hooked finger, my flame.

LITTLE PARABLE FOR DOORS

"As long as we're here, let's go next door" or
"since we're here, let's walk right across"
is the same as
"we might as well" which means
as long as we're here
we might also be
standing somewhere else. Over there.
And as expected, one of the group
would like to stand somewhere else.
As long as two doorways
stand shoulder to shoulder,
and here might as well be there,
the group shrugs, why not,
and crosses over.

And next door, a tame finch with an orange beak,
a rose in glass, caught and suspended,
something rare, exquisite
might soon be lost or sold.
It's the possibility
of never coming here again,
(and therefore, never there)
that urges the group next door.
The day there might grow longer,
merchants' shelves pile themselves higher.
The rounded cobbles ring as never before when crossed.
Of course, it's just an intuition, a tone,
a slight threat one makes to oneself,
but it serves the walk next door.

One casts herself next door
like a penny in a fountain,
a shining weight that rocks and settles
back to back with others, promising return.
Casts across the loaves of cobbles, straddles indecision,
the little darkness of an alley. One might find
the door there locked, or then again
find a bird cast up in song,
a rose more beautiful than any other
and everything suddenly worth the trip.

Of course, it might be
illustrated this way too:
imagine one is angry at herself,
at a mistake she's made and distracted
(considering far better ripostes)
trips and falls down the stairs.
Now as long as she's upset,
has fallen down the stairs,
why not toss herself out a window
if she's feeling bad enough?

Clearly the shadows of both propositions,
moving *here* to *there* and moving *stair* to *window*
cast themselves out at absurdly different lengths,
seem so ill-matched as to deny comparison
and also appear intolerable.

Yet, if even one member of the group
is looking skyward toward the window,
is in an agreeable state of mind or is herself distracted,
knows little geography, how far or near the next door is.
fears she will never return, believes only the present,
believes her time or good fortune's nearly up,

she will climb higher as if led by the hand
believe the solid clouds, fall
and think it an entirely
different feeling this time, and worth it,
a rose in one hand, in the other
a tiny, breathless bird.

ANDREI RUBLEV

(icon painter, ca. 1370-1430)

Riding across these days, expanses,
pinpoint stars, rushes
before peasants bind them, yellow
sweating off the bundles,

I plough with the hooves
of my white horse, forward, red-oxide,
a rind of cheese in my pocket.

I am Andrei when nothing of the sky
discloses the origins of its color
and still I am he
when I touch the gold
kept in mind
for the head of St. Peter.
I walk on scaffolding
to reach the cathedral's high walls.

I touch the arc of a horse's tail
held at a distance from his body
like the tassel on a royal robe
knotted in the style of the age.

I am Andrei the way my whole journey
appears to you, in flattened pictures
moving across your vision like a story.

Andrei, the way light shrinks
through slats in a dark house,

the way I dream my crimes
will be tried—
as nothing
to God, everything
to me hovering, preparing
the surface with gesso, canvas,
gesso, leaf, egg.

I am Andrei threading white
through the eyelet sleeve of Michael.

Over the steppes I am
a wash of belief, an ocher sandstorm
that would be pollen
sifting from my fruit trees
had I stayed home.

I am Andrei the way applause
is concealed in sap
for decades, then bursts
into rustling, gathered
and stirring now
in the folds and shadows cast
by their garments, I hope.

Viewer,
I am Andrei in your absence
before you and after
and when you stop looking.

I run my fingers
along hems and crowns
to mark a place for amethyst,

to measure
the likely radiance.

I keep the colors in my bag—
dried yolk for sun, crushed
stalks beaten silver and for sky
a thin rain of red and vine-leaf.
I am interrupted at my work,
it will not leave me.

In the dirt beneath my nails I am
he who scraped along the bone
of a holy face with black
to make it holier to all,

and he who pulled the eyes forward,
twisted the head
so those who stand below
might feel the gaze
naturally inclined towards them.

I am Andrei eating bread,
the slope, length, heft
of it swallowed at once.

Andrei, with a knife, already knitting
light over the head I, just this morning,
laid on the wet board as shadow.

Andrei—I cannot believe it myself
this name I put to the work I was given,
I who cannot finish on time
whose patrons shake loud coins in my ears.

Andrei, one step ahead of the Tatars,
dark riders whose faces
I turn to see,
faces like those of my saints,
without dimension in the driving wind,
eyes closed against the dust, searching
inside their century,

Andrei, the way I clear for them.

LETTER

Dear,
no one I ever knew
plucked the jewel from the eye of the captor
threw it away
and thus knew freedom.

Got up early today.
Saw first that edelweiss on the wall
still ugly behind glass.
Rare though, many fingers.
Snow melted in the crook of a tree last night
and stained the bark black.
Collected rags to wash.
Wished for replacement rags for work.
Left a red pepper two days
on the sill. Seeds dried
and lightened the whole room
considerably.